for Goldie 🐾

For more lessons & activities about dogs, visit:
www.ilikedogs.org

Published by Four Foot Press LLC   www.fourfootpress.com

Text copyright © Debra Cheehy 2009
Illustrations copyright © Carol Hilliard 2009

Cheehy, Debra.

I like dogs / by Debra Cheehy ; illustrated by Carol Hilliard. – 1st ed.
– Manassas, Va. : Four Foot Press, c2009.

p. ; cm.
ISBN: 978-0-9820817-0-9
Audience: Ages 5-9.
Summary: A follow-the-action educational trip to the animal shelter
teaches children compassion for homeless pets. The book introduces
children to different dog breeds and illustrates how their talents
benefit us all. The reader is encouraged to "make a difference"
in their own community.

1. Dogs–Juvenile literature. 2. Pet adoption–Juvenile literature.
3. Animal shelters–Juvenile literature. 4. Dog breeds–Juvenile literature.
5. [Dogs. 6. Pet adoption. 7. Animal shelters. 8. Stories in rhyme.]
I. Hilliard, Carol. II. Title.

SF426.5 .C44 2009   2008935533
636.7–dc22   0901

ACKNOWLEDGEMENTS
Edited by Jason Cheehy
Book Design by Carol Hilliard

Bloodhound, *Ruby* CA rescue   photo by Diana Ryan
Dachshund, *Fritz* TX rescue   photo by Debra Martinez
Dalmatian, *Molly* VA rescue   photo by Terri McGilvray
German Shepherd Dog, *Moxy* VA rescue   photo by Steve Cheehy
Labrador Retriever, *Army* VA rescue   photo by Steve Cheehy
Newfoundland, *Penny* PA   photo by Laurie Thomas
Old English Sheepdog, *Wilby* FL rescue   photo by Carol Mahler
Sleeve Pekingese, *Goldie* TX rescue   photo by Steve Cheehy

Our rescued dogs love **MULTIPET INTERNATIONAL** toys!

In kind memory of Laury Estrada and her rescued Doberman Zeus.
Thank you Julie ~ C.H.

I like dogs

by Debra Cheehy

illustrated by Carol Hilliard

CALL OF THE WILD

SOUNDER

OLD YELLER

LASSIE COME HOME

THE INCREDIBLE JOURNEY

RIN TIN TIN AND RUSTY

Hello!
My name is Amanda May.
I like dogs!
I think I'll get one today!

I will go to the shelter
and **not** the pet store.

I know the dogs there
need a family **MUCH** more.

"I am here for a dog, no particular kind. May I look in the cages to see what I'll find?
There are **so many** dogs. They all look so sad.
Why are they here?   Are they lost?
WERE THEY BAD?"

"Oh no!
They're not bad," said dog warden Laury.
"Let's look at the dogs while I tell you their story.

All of these dogs were lost or brought in...
by their owner, a person they **thought** was their friend."

Their owners had reasons that **THEY** thought were good:
"We're moving...
He's old...
I should train him, I should.

Won't you please take him? My kids are all grown.
At least he'll be here...
and not home alone."

"We take them all in, and then do our best.
Some will find homes,
but it's sad for the rest.

They spend their time waiting
in cages ALL day.

So please look around and

ADOPT ONE
TODAY!"

Dog
Treats

LOST!

"Liz"

$10 Reward

Plea

eek

Eight dogs in cages, some **BIG** and some small.

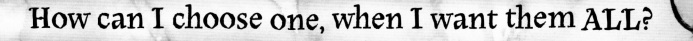

How can I choose one, when I want them ALL?

I look at their faces and sigh, now decided.

I WILL RESCUE THEM ALL.
I am so excited!

I have a new family to love and to care for,
to feed and to pet and always be there for.
I'll fill out the papers then be on my way.

Oh, what a special,
spectacular day!

I'll take you all home,
then I'll go to the store.
I have to buy dog stuff
and DOG FOOD
GALORE.

But as we walk on,
I hear a voice in the park.
"**HELP!**
I can't find my son! His name is MARK.
He had been playing right here. I told him to stay.
Mark lost his shoe when he wandered away."

Just then my puppy,
the floppy Bloodhound,
jumps out of my arms and
onto the ground.

He sniffs the boy's shoe
then runs off with a

BARK.

A few minutes later...

...that dog has FOUND MARK!

Mark's mom is amazed at this magnificent hound.
What a wonderful friend little Mark has just found!

She reaches to scratch the brown dog on his head,
with a wink and a smile, turns to me and then says,

"You look like you have a dog extra (or two!). Please let us have him...

We love him. We do!"

I do have **8** dogs, some **BIG** and some small.
They were left and forgotten so **I rescued them ALL.**
So if you want him and feel up to the task,
there are just a few questions I feel I *must* ask...

Will you promise not to leave him, in the rain or the cold?

Will you love him forever, even when he is old?

Will you feed him and pet him every single day?

Will you always be there and ready to play?

Will he live in the house alongside of you?

Will you train him to know what he shouldn't do?

Will you be his best friend for as long as he lives?

And take all the love he so eagerly gives?

If **ALL** of these things you can **promise to me,**
then take your new puppy.
It was meant to be.

Mark holds his new puppy real close to his chest,
saying, "Yes, yes I promise, I will do **MY BEST.**
I'll do what you ask, and then I'll do more.
**I'll love him forever and
then evermore."**

So I promise to visit and try not to cry.
I pray he'll be loved as I kiss him good-bye.

At the lake in the distance, I see a commotion.
The Newfoundland looks up,
and then... *she's in motion!*

She jumps in the lake as quick as a wink.
She saves the young man before he can sink.

The man hugs her neck and thanks her sincerely,
"This dog **SAVED MY LIFE,** and I love her dearly.

I would love to have her for my very own.
She would be my best friend and have a great home."

I have **7** dogs, some **BIG** and some small. They were left and forgotten so I rescued them ALL.
I'll have **6** dogs to love if I give her to you.

But first, *there are some things you must promise to do...*

So I ask him my questions and await his reply.
With a prayer, pat, and promise... I then say goodbye.

We continue our journey on past a farm.
The sheep are out running and heading for harm.
The gate was left open. That's how they got out.
"Hurry and herd them,
old sheepdog!" I shout.

She runs
BACK+FORTH
to get them in line,
then drives them back home
in world record time.

The farmer comes out to see what is up,
saying, "You saved my sheep,
you wonderful
PUP!

I sure need a dog
to help with these sheep,
**A dog I could love,
care for and keep."**

I do have **6** dogs, some **BIG** and some small.
They were left and forgotten so I rescued them **ALL**.
I'll have **5** dogs to love if I give her to you.
But first, *there are some things you must promise to do...*
So I ask him my questions and await his reply.   With a prayer, pat, and promise I then say goodbye.

Then down the street I start once more,
when one of the dogs begins to explore.

The little red dachshund goes **left** ... and then, **right**.
Up to a porch, ... and then out of sight.

He is **sniffing**
and **scratching**
at something he's found.

It's something
VERY tiny
hiding
under
the ground.

The little girl questions
as she comes outside,

"**what is he doing?**

Is he trying to HIDE?"

I say,
"He's found
SOMETHING!
Do you know
what it IS...?"

"I have been looking for her
for the last several days.
She escaped through a hole
in her exercise maze.

Thank you sweet dog,
I'm so glad she's been found.
Now she can go back to her cage
safe and sound.

I love this dog,
he's so cute and so smart.
If he were mine,
we never would part."

"If I ask my mom,

and she should agree...

...Would you please, could you please,

Give him to me?"

I do have **5** dogs, some **BIG** and some small.
They were left and forgotten so I rescued them ALL.

I'll have **4** dogs to love if I give him to you.
But first, *there are some things you must promise to do...*

I ask her my questions and await her reply. With a prayer, pat, and promise I then say goodbye.

A fire truck catches the spotted dog's eye.
The fireman looks like a really nice guy.
The dog runs right up for a pat on the head. The fireman greets him.
Here's what is said...

"We sure need a mascot at this fire station.

We would love to have
this handsome Dalmatian.

Most stations have one. We want one, too.

We will all love him.

We already do!"

I do have 4 dogs, some BIG and some small.
They were left and forgotten so I rescued them ALL.
I'll have 3 dogs to love if I give him to you.
But first, *there are some things you must promise to do...*

So I ask them my questions and await their reply.   With a prayer, pat, and promise I then say goodbye.

Only two blocks to go, we're almost there.
Ahead, see the girl with pretty blonde hair.
She has just dropped her bag onto the ground.
The Labrador retrieves it, that very smart hound.
He puts the bag gently back on her lap.
She says to him sweetly,
"You're quite a **fine** chap!"

"Along with the tender love that he brings,
he could **assist me** with everyday things.
I'd love to have this wonderful guy.

We'd make a GREAT TEAM, just he and I."

I do have **3** dogs, some **BIG** and some small. They were left and forgotten so I rescued them ALL.

I'll have **2** dogs to love if I give him to you.   But first, *there are some things you must promise to do...*

So I ask her my questions and await her reply. With a prayer, pat, and promise I then say goodbye.

What is that sound that's piercing the air?
It seems to be coming from right over there.

It's the alarm from the jewelry store.
LOOK! There's a man running out of the door!

Trying to catch him,
the policeman
gives chase...

The German Shepherd takes off.
THERE'S NO TIME TO WASTE!

He catches up swiftly
then grabs the man's arm.
He holds him there **bravely**
while doing no harm.

Now quickly comes
**Officer Joe to
the scene...**

Saying,
**"WoW! What a dog.
Boy, is he
keen!"**

"I bet we could **train** him to **help with our work**, patrolling the places where **bad people lurk**."

I have only **2** dogs, one **BIG** and one small.

On my way home, **I FOUND HOMES FOR THEM ALL!**

I'll have **1** dog to love if I give him to you.

But first,

there are some things you must promise to do...

So I ask him my questions and await his reply.

With a prayer, pat, and promise I then say goodbye.

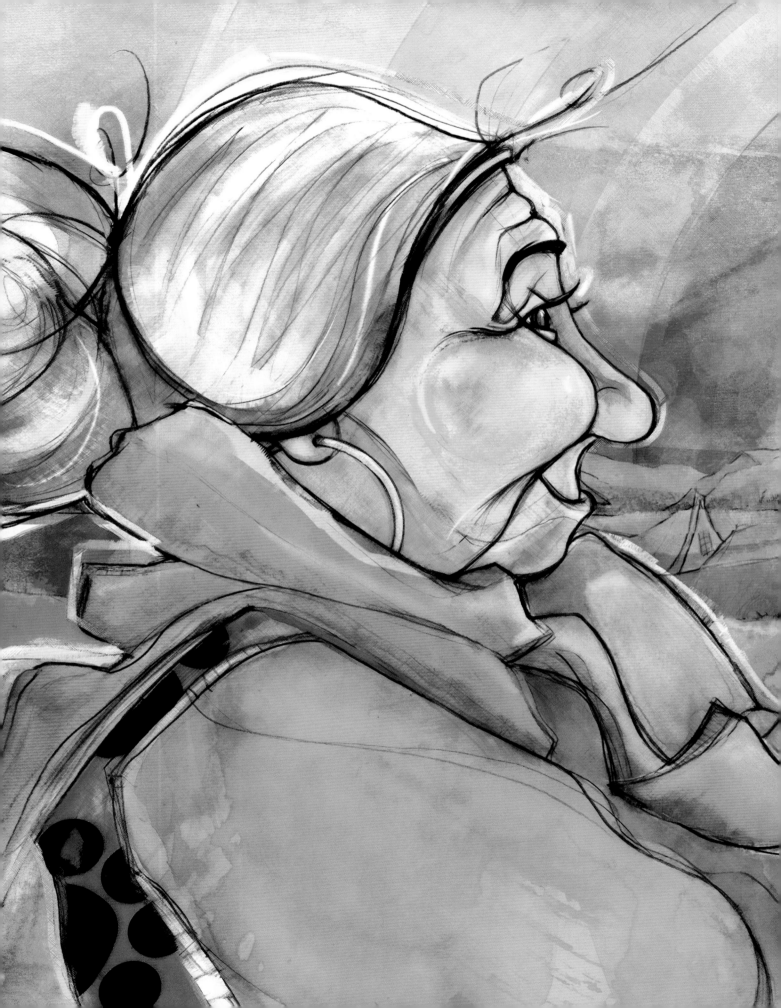

Now you are the only dog left just for me,
My Pekingese mix, as cute as can be!

Although you're not any particular breed,
you're PERFECT to give me the love that I need.

The others are gone, but we won't be sad.
They all have great homes and we should be glad.
I know we will miss them,
but I have a plan...

We will visit them ALL
as soon as we CAN!

Every Saturday,
we will **meet at the park**,
where all of you dogs can
run, play
and
BARK!

AND...

We will go to the shelter at least once a week.
We will take all the dogs the shelter can't keep.
They will **ALL** live with us and we will have fun,

'Til we find the right home
for every last one.

Come sit on my lap.
Let me hold you tight.
I have something to say; it's only right.
The promise that I asked of everyone today,
is a promise that I should be willing to say.

I will not leave you out in the rain or the cold.

I will love you forever, even when you are old.

I will feed you and pet you every single day.

I will always be there and ready to play.

I will keep you in the house alongside of me.

I will train you so you will behave properly.

I will be your best friend for as long as you live.

I will take all the love you so eagerly give.

Now you need a name.
Oh what will it be?
I know. Of course, I will call you **Goldie!**

Our busy day is done. I guess that is that.
Oh no! I've just realized...
I also like cats!

Now, if **YOU** like dogs...

1. Adopt a Pet

Over 12 million dogs and cats are abandoned each year.

ALWAYS SPAY OR NEUTER YOUR PET!

CATS

2. Volunteer

Many shelters and rescues are run by volunteers and need your helping hands!

3. Sponsor a Fundraiser

Bake Sale
Garage Sale
Penny Drive
Paper Drive
Pet Parade
Car Wash
Dog Wash

5 Things You Can Do to Help!

4. Foster a Pet

Just like Amanda, you can provide a temporary home until a homeless pet finds its forever family.

5. Donate to Your Local Shelter or Breed Rescue

Call first to see what is needed most. Here are some ideas:

Food	Blankets	Beds	Cat Litter
Collars	Leashes	Dishes	Carriers
Kennels	Newspapers	Baby Gates	Dog Houses

Monetary donations are always welcome!

"Wilby"
Old English Sheepdog

"Moxy"
German Shepherd Dog

"Goldie"
Sleeve Pekingese

"Ruby"
Bloodhound

"Molly" Dalmatian

"Army"
Labrador
Retriever

If You Are Thinking of Adopting, Please Remember:

No matter what breed you decide on,
all dogs need training to bring out their natural abilities.

Please do research to make sure your new dog
will be the right dog for your family.

Always check your local shelter and breed rescue groups;
they are sure to have a large assortment of dogs
waiting for a loving home.

Just like the dogs you've read about,
the rescued dogs pictured here have
all found their forever homes!

"Fritz" Dachshund

"Penny"
Newfoundland

Can you guess the breed by reading the rhyme?

Try to figure it out before the last line!

I have short legs, but long ears and long snout.
If you're a badger, you better watch out!
I'll sniff and I'll follow you under the ground.
In German, my name means badger hound.
I look like something you eat on a bun.
A German scent hound, I'm the little Dachshund.

I will go for a hunt or help you to see.
Whatever you need, you can count on me.
I'm a beautiful dog — chocolate, yellow, or black.
If you throw me something, I'll bring it right back.
A sporting dog from Newfoundland in spite of my name,
I'm a Labrador Retriever: please throw it again!

I'm big, and I'm furry and have webbed feet.
I love to swim in the blue and the deep.
If you fall in the water, I'll jump right in;
I'll get you to shore and be your best friend.
I'm a working dog, but I still like to have fun.
I'm a Newfoundland and that's where I'm from.

I am born all white, but get spots as I grow.
I've been trail hound, coach dog, and star of the show.
A dog from Dalmatia that gave me my name,
Protecting fire trucks is my favorite game.
So look for me at your fire station;
A non-sporting dog, I'm a Dalmatian.

I am big and floppy and have a loud bark.
I love to go on long walks in the park.
I'll track you by scent instead of by sight,
That means I can find you even at night!
So if you are lost and you need to be found,
Call the scent hound from Germany,
The trusty Bloodhound.

I'm small and I'm furry. I have a flat face.
A palace in Peking is my favorite place.
If I'm really tiny they call me a sleeve;
That's where empress carried me, so I wouldn't leave.
A lion-hearted dog, an imp if you please,
A toy dog from China, the imperial Pekingese.

I'm big and I'm shaggy, a keeper of sheep.
If I were your dog, on your bed I would sleep.
My breed's old and it's English, I work till the end.
I'm an Old English Sheepdog. Can I be your friend?

I've helped with the military and police dressed in blue.
I've been guide dog protector, but here's the best clue:
I'm a worker from Germany, a shepherd of sheep,
The German Shepherd Dog; I'll keep guard while you sleep.

I can be BIG, or I can be small.
I can be any color,
any color
at all.

I am able
to love you,
just like the rest.
If you try to teach me,
I will do
my best.

I am
unique,
that's what I am told,
I'm a MIXED BREED with a heart of pure gold.

To print out your very own certificate, go to www.ilikedogs.org

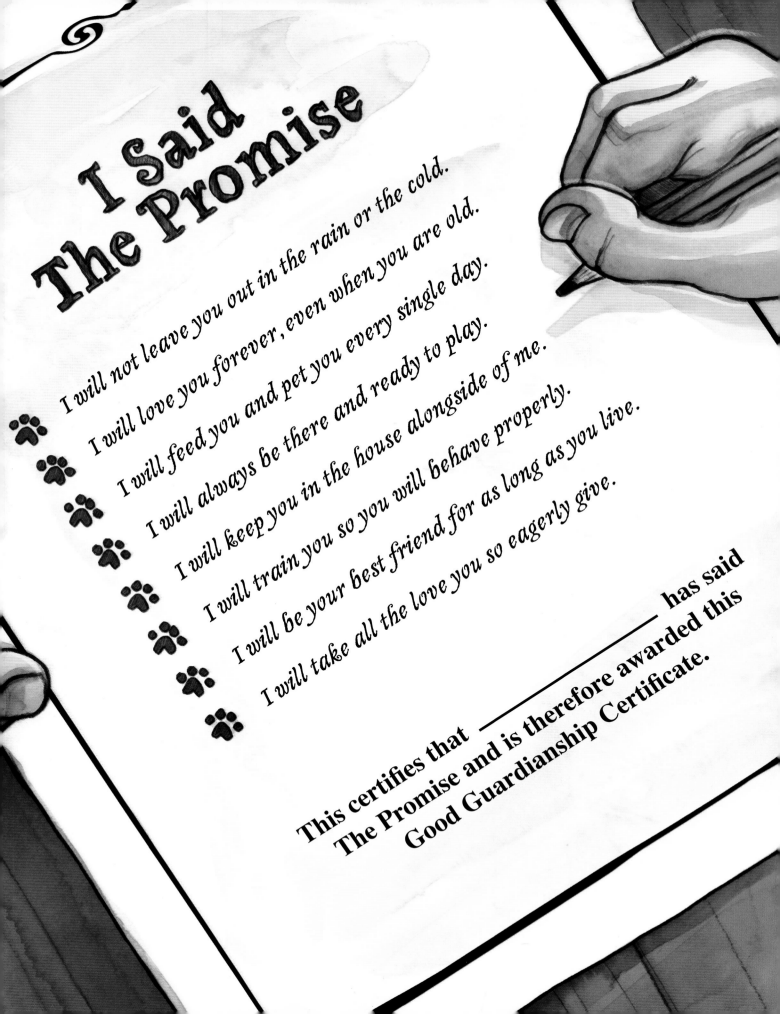

I Said The Promise

I will not leave you out in the rain or the cold.

I will love you forever, even when you are old.

I will feed you and pet you every single day.

I will always be there and ready to play.

I will keep you in the house alongside of me.

I will train you so you will behave properly.

I will be your best friend for as long as you live.

I will take all the love you so eagerly give.

This certifies that _____ has said The Promise and is therefore awarded this Good Guardianship Certificate.

As you see,
dogs are useful to child, beast and man.
In return, **shouldn't we help them any way that we can?**

If everyone who wanted a pet could agree, to ALL of these promises I'm sure that we'd see. . .
a world better for all, person and pet.
We're getting better, **but we're not there yet.**

Will you help
with my dream of a
home for them **ALL?**
Please make a promise,
no matter how small.

Do SOMETHING to help
all these babies in fur ~
**You can
make a difference!**
I know that for sure.

That is my story, and
thank you for reading.
Now go on, get started.
**Go do some
GOOD DEEDING!**

The End